LEVEL ONE
Adult Piano Theory
47 Programmed Lessons

by

David Carr Glover

FOREWORD

This book reinforces the fundamentals of music being studied in the Adult Piano Student — Level One by David Carr Glover. It consists of 47 Programmed Theory Lessons. The material for each lesson is divided into steps called "frames." Many of the same frames are presented several times for review thus reinforcing fundamentals already presented.

When this book has been successfully completed, the student will be prepared to play, understand, and enjoy music at this level of advancement.

All three levels in this series may also be used with any other course of study.

Materials Correlated with The Adult Piano Student — Level I

Lesson No. 1

The keyboard has black and white keys. The black keys are divided into groups of twos and threes.

With a pencil circle all groups of two black keys.

With a pencil circle all groups of three black keys.

Complete the following sentences using the words Up or Down.

This way ——→ is _____Up_____ on the keyboard.

This way ←—— is _____Down_____ on the keyboard.

Complete the following sentences using the words High or Low.

_____High_____ tones are up to the right of Middle C.

_____Low_____ tones are down to the left of Middle C.

This ≣≣≣ is a STAFF.

How many lines does a staff have? _____5_____

How many spaces does a staff have? _____4_____

FDL 737

Lesson No. 2

The LINES of a music staff are numbered from the bottom to the top.

Counting from the bottom up to the top write the number name for the LINE notes below.

5 2 4 1 3 L 2 4 5 3 1 5

The SPACES of a music staff are numbered from the bottom to the top.

Counting from the bottom up to the top write the number name for the SPACE notes below.

3 4 1 2 3 1 2 4 1 2 3 4

Notes are placed on the staff with LINES through them -●- or in SPACES ＸＯＸ .
Using Whole Notes ○ draw the LINE notes indicated. Count from the bottom up to the top.

1 3 2 5 4 1 4 3 5 2 1 5

Using Whole Notes ○ draw the SPACE notes indicated. Count from the bottom up to the top.

2 4 1 2 3 4 1 3 4 2 1 3

Using Whole Notes ○ draw the LINE and SPACE notes indicated.

2S 1L 5L 4S 3L 1S 5L 2L 2S 3S 2L 4L

FDL 737

Lesson No. 3

NOTES on the music staff indicate what keys to play. They move UP, DOWN, and REPEAT.

Under the following pairs of NOTES write U when they move <u>up</u>, D when they move <u>down</u>, and R when they repeat.

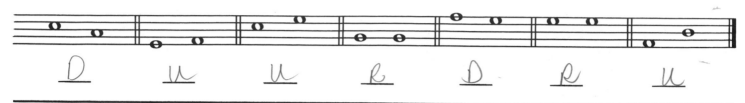

D   U   U   R   D   R   U

The MUSIC ALPHABET uses the following letter names: A B C D E F G. This alphabet is repeated over and over again on the white keys of the keyboard.

How many letter names are there in a Music Alphabet? ___7___

They are ___A B C D E F G___ .

On the following white keys write letter names to complete the two Music Alphabets. The first letter name is given for each.

A B C D E F G A B C D E F G

Write letter names on all white keys marked with an X.

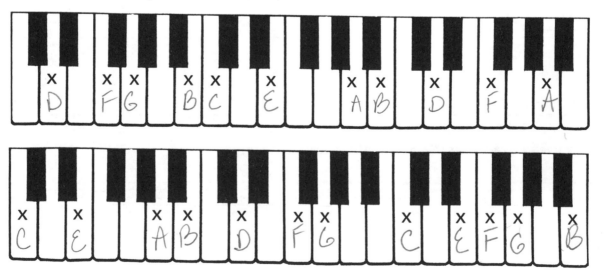

X D   X F   X G   X B   X C   X E   X A   X B   X D   X F   X A

X C   X E   X A   X B   X D   X F   X G   X C   X E   X F   X G   X B

Lesson No. 4

Very old letters, called CLEF SIGNS, are used at the beginning of each musical staff to name two special lines, F and G.

F CLEF
or
BASS CLEF

This clef names the 4th line F. It is the first F below the middle of your keyboard. Your Left Hand will usually play the notes on this staff.

Draw four F Clef (Bass Clef) signs.

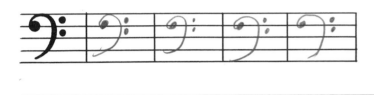

G CLEF
or
TREBLE CLEF

This clef names the 2nd line G. It is the first G above the middle of your keyboard. Your Right Hand will usually play the notes on this staff.

Draw four G Clef (Treble Clef) signs.

The following is a GRAND STAFF. It is joined together with a BRACE and is divided into MEASURES by BAR LINES. At the end of a piece of music a DOUBLE BAR is used.

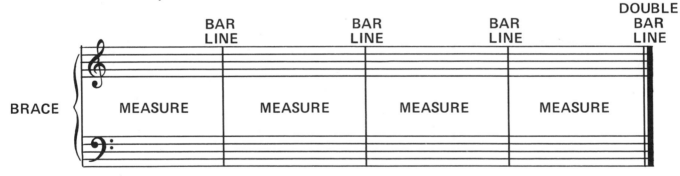

Copy the above Grand Staff below.

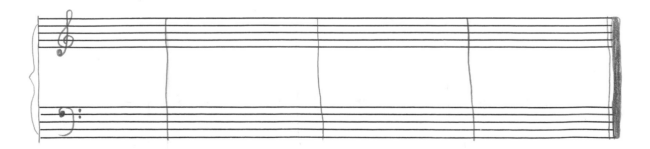

6

Lesson No. 5

The letter names of the TREBLE STAFF LINE NOTES are E G B D F. They form alphabet skips. The white keys they represent on the keyboard form key skips.

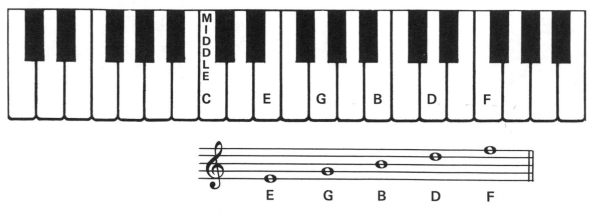

Write the correct letter names for the following Treble Staff Line Notes.

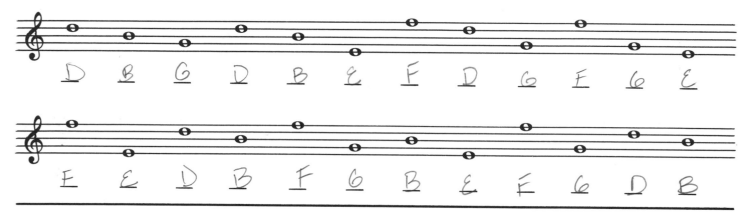

D B G D B E F D G E G E

E E D B F G B E E F G D B

Draw the correct Treble Staff Line Notes above the given letter names. Use Whole Notes.

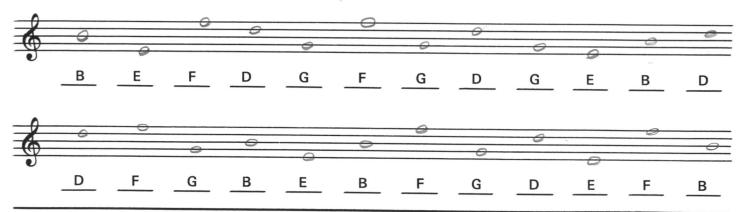

B E F D G F G D G E B D

D F G B E B F G D E F B

Write the correct letter names for the following Treble Staff Line Notes. They spell words.

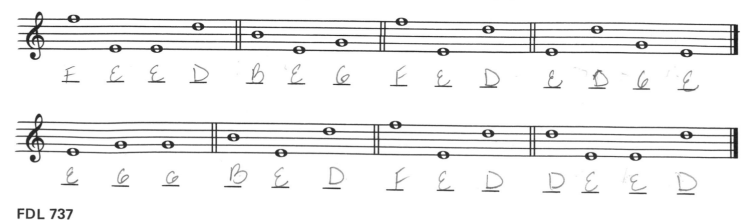

E E E D B E G F E D E D G E

E G G B E D F E D D E E D

Lesson No. 6

The letter names of the TREBLE STAFF SPACE NOTES are F A C E. They form alphabet skips. The white keys they represent on the keyboard form key skips.

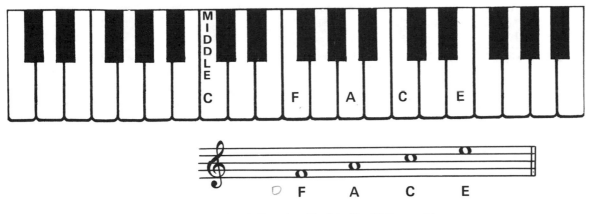

Write the correct letter names for the following Treble Staff Space Notes.

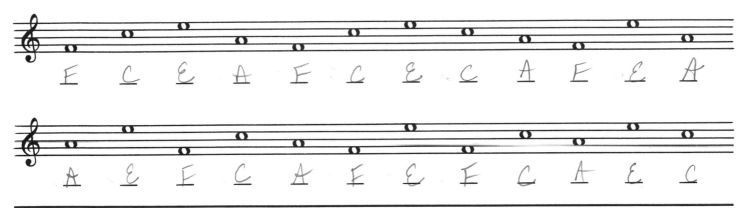

Draw the correct Treble Staff Space Notes above the given letter names. Use Whole Notes.

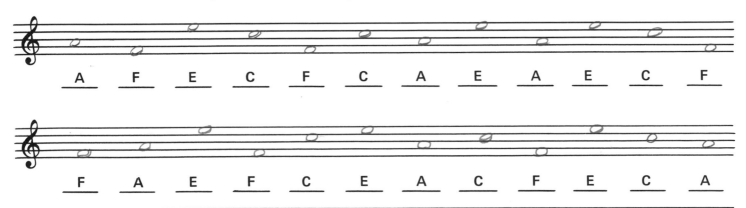

Write the correct letter names for the following Treble Staff Space Notes. They spell words.

FDL 737

8

Lesson No. 7

The letter names of the BASS STAFF LINE NOTES are G B D F A. They form alphabet skips. The white keys they represent on the keyboard form key skips.

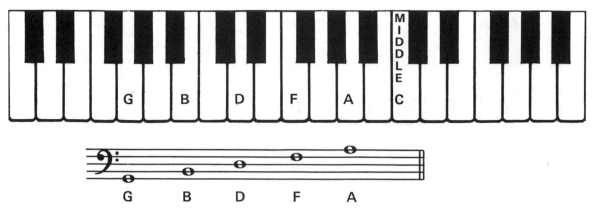

Write the correct letter names for the following Bass Staff Line Notes.

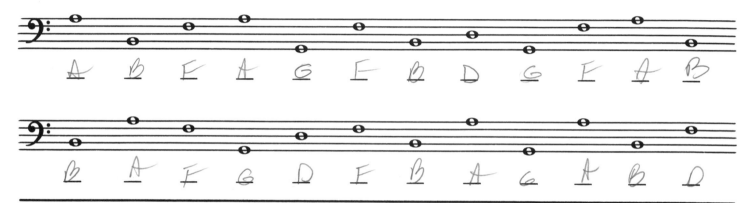

A B E A G E B D G E A B

B A F G D E B A G A B D

Draw the correct Bass Staff Line Notes above the given letter names. Use Whole Notes.

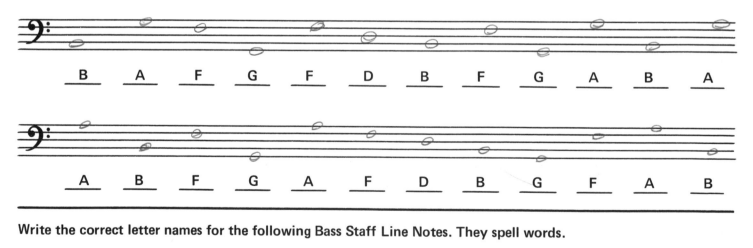

B A F G F D B F G A B A

A B F G A F D B G F A B

Write the correct letter names for the following Bass Staff Line Notes. They spell words.

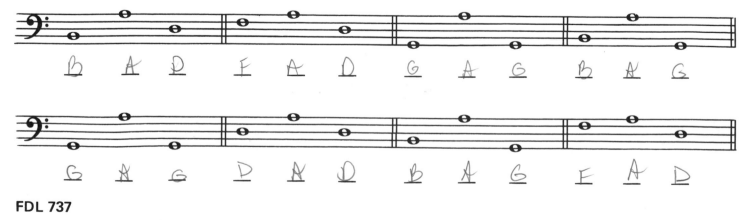

B A D E A D G A G B A G

G A G D A D B A G E A D

FDL 737

Lesson No. 8

The letter names of the BASS STAFF SPACE NOTES are A C E G. They form alphabet skips. The white keys they represent on the keyboard form key skips.

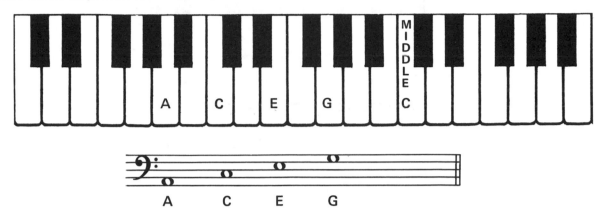

Write the correct letter names for the following Bass Staff Space Notes.

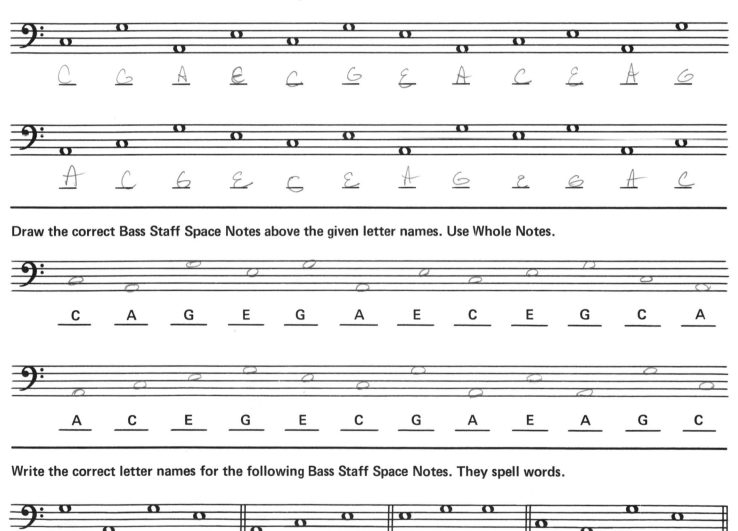

Draw the correct Bass Staff Space Notes above the given letter names. Use Whole Notes.

Write the correct letter names for the following Bass Staff Space Notes. They spell words.

FDL 737

Lesson No. 9

Notes and keys ABOVE
Bass Staff and BELOW
Treble Staff.

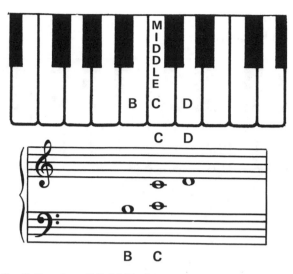

Write the correct letter names for the following GRAND STAFF notes.

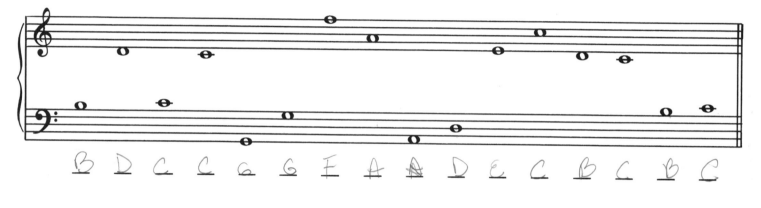

B D C C G G E A A D E C B C B C

 The top number of this TIME or METER SIGNATURE indicates TWO beats in each measure. The bottom number indicates each QUARTER NOTE receives ONE beat.

Draw four ⅔ Time or Meter Signatures on the staff below.

This ♩ is a QUARTER NOTE. It receives ONE beat
when the ⅔ Time or Meter Signature is used.

Draw four Quarter Notes like the one given.

This ♩ is a HALF NOTE. It receives TWO beats
when the ⅔ Time or Meter Signature is used.

Draw four Half Notes like the one given.

Lesson No. 10

The letter names of the GRAND STAFF LINES and SPACES are:

G A B C D E F G A B C D E F G A B C D E F

The letter names of the GRAND STAFF LINES form alphabet skips. They are:

G — B — D — F — A — C — E — G — B — D — F

The white keys they represent on the keyboard form key skips. On the white keys marked X write the correct letter names.

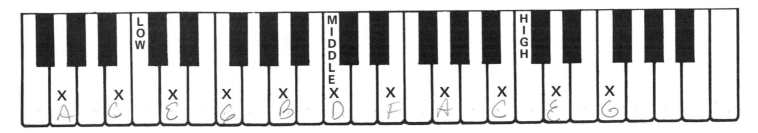

Write letter names for the following GRAND STAFF LINE notes.

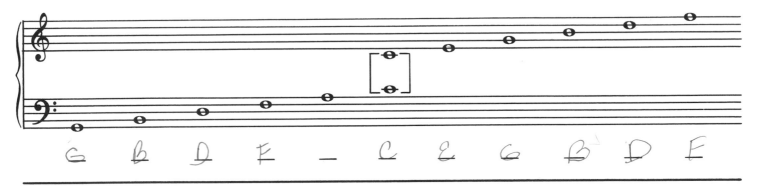

G G B D F _ C E G B D E

  The top number of this TIME or METER SIGNATURE indicates THREE beats in each measure. The bottom number indicates each QUARTER NOTE receives ONE beat.

Draw four $\frac{3}{4}$ Time or Meter Signatures on the staff below.

This ♩ is a QUARTER NOTE. It receives ONE beat when the $\frac{3}{4}$ Time or Meter Signature is used.

Draw four Quarter Notes like the one given.

This ♩ is a HALF NOTE. It receives TWO beats when the $\frac{3}{4}$ Time or Meter Signature is used.

Draw four Half Notes like the one given.

This ♩. is a DOTTED HALF NOTE. It receives THREE beats when the $\frac{3}{4}$ Time or Meter Signature is used.

Draw four Dotted Half Notes like the one given.

Lesson No. 11

The letter names of the GRAND STAFF LINES and SPACES are:

G A B C D E F G A B C D E F G A B C D E F

The letter names of the GRAND STAFF SPACES form alphabet skips. They are:

A – C – E – G – B – D – F – A – C – E

The white keys they represent on the keyboard form key skips. On the white keys marked X write the correct letter names.

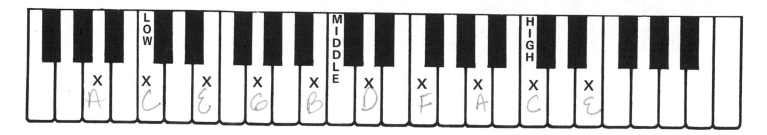

Write letter names for the following GRAND STAFF SPACE notes.

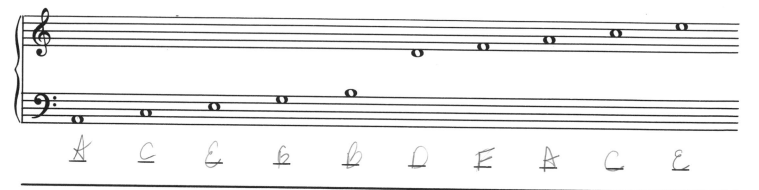

A   C   E   G   B   D   E   A   C   E

 The top number of this TIME or METER SIGNATURE indicates FOUR beats in each measure. The bottom number indicates each QUARTER NOTE receives ONE beat.

Draw four **4/4** Time or Meter Signatures on the staff below.

This **o** is a WHOLE NOTE. It receives FOUR beats when the **4/4** Time or Meter Signature is used.

Draw four Whole Notes like the one given.

Write the number of beats each of the following notes receive in **4/4** Time or Meter.

1   2   4   3

Lesson No. 12

Identify by name the following notes.

whole quater dotted half half

All notes, except Whole Notes, have stems. Up stems are on the RIGHT side of a note. Draw UP stems to the following notes.

Down stems are on the LEFT side of a note. Draw DOWN stems to the following notes.

When the note is on or above the middle line of the staff the stem goes DOWN on the left.

When the note is below the middle line of the staff the stem goes UP on the right.

Draw stems on the following note heads.

Change the following notes as indicated.

QUARTER NOTE ¼ = ♩

HALF NOTE ½ = 𝅗𝅥

DOTTED HALF NOTE ½. = 𝅗𝅥.

½ ¼ ½. ¼ ½ ½. ¼ ½ ¼ ½.

¼ ½. ½ ¼ ½ ½. ¼ ½. ½ ½.

Lesson No. 13

This ⅃ is a QUARTER REST. It receives ONE beat when the ²⁄₄, ³⁄₄, or ⁴⁄₄ Time or Meter Signature is used.

Draw four Quarter Rests.

This ▬ is a HALF REST. It receives TWO beats when the ²⁄₄, ³⁄₄, or ⁴⁄₄ Time or Meter Signature is used.

Draw four Half Rests.

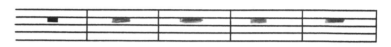

This ▬ is a WHOLE MEASURE REST. It receives FOUR beats when the ⁴⁄₄ Time or Meter Signature is used. It receives THREE beats when the ³⁄₄ Time or Meter Signature is used.

Draw four Whole Measure Rests.

Add TIME SIGNATURES to each line of music.

Using BAR LINES divide the following music into measures. Write in the beat counts for each measure. The first measure is given.

FDL 737

UCI

SYMPHONY

ORCHESTRA

The evening started just after sunset as the audience were ushered to their seats, in this small but elegant theatre. The orchestra began to tune and warm-up their instruments and themselves. There was no curtain to draw so the opening of the symphony was started with the seating of the players, as the audience and the symphony waited expectantly for Jerzy Kosek, the conductor to arrive and begin the evening filled with Ludwig van Beethoven. The program was arranged intelligently, opening with Overture to Egmont Op. 84-Sostenuto, ma non troppo; allegro. I found this piece to be very captivating, it kept my attention throughout the entire piece. The conductor was very energetic and he was enjoyable to watch. This introduction to the symphony had a Spanish rhythm, I was constantly tapping my foot throughout this piece. At times I wanted to get up and dance. It was so thrilling to see the music live, rather than merely hearing it. The way that the orchestra is set up is to fulfill the sense of sight. I was never bored watching the violins that were right up front, all of their movements were exciting to watch. In the center up front was of course the conductor. On the opposite side of the violins were placed the cello and other stringed instruments. By the time the first piece was over I couldn't wait to hear what was in store for me in the next piece which included the piano for the first time this evening. The piano was placed in front of the orchestra and the conductor, I don't understand why it was placed where it was. I guess when the piano comes into play the rest of the orchestra including the conductor is down staged. Luckily from my point of view in the theatre I could still see the conductor, the unfortunate others seated in the middle and

right side could not. I was fortunate to be seated on the keyboard side of the piano. Piano conerto no. 1 in C major, op. 15 was my first experience of piano in concert and after this one will definitely not be my last. Lucerne DeSa was the extraordinary pianist for the evening, it was inspiring to watch her hands glide across the keys with such ease and elegance yet at the same time with the authority to command the orchestra and the audience. The way in which the orchestra come in and out with the piano was ingenious, which is not uncommon with Beethoven. I really enjoyed how the conductor and pianist related to one another in the course of the piece. This piece finished with a marvelous climax from the piano and orchestra together and a standing ovation was in order for the performance of Ms. DeSa. After an experience as this an intermission was placed strategically. After the intermission we were brought back into the nineteenth century with Beethoven as we sit at his fourth symphony in Bb major, op. 60. The themes of this piece are cheerful and light-hearted. The piece starts out calmly and goes into a fast and ornamented section and then when your not expection it your right back into a soft flowing section with the strings and at that moment you realize it, one last burst of energy to top off o memorable eve in the theatre with Ludwig van Beethoven.

Lesson No. 14

A short curved line over  or under a group of notes is called a SLUR. All notes in the group are to be played LEGATO (smooth and connected).

Add a SLUR line ABOVE each group of notes. The first one is given.

Add a SLUR line BELOW each group of notes. The first one is given.

An INTERVAL is the distance between two notes. Count the letter names of the lines and spaces between the two notes and include the given lowest and highest notes.

Prime (Unison)   2nd   3rd   4th   5th   6th   7th   8th (Octave)

The above notes are played together. They are called HARMONIC INTERVALS.

Write NUMBER NAMES for the following HARMONIC INTERVALS.

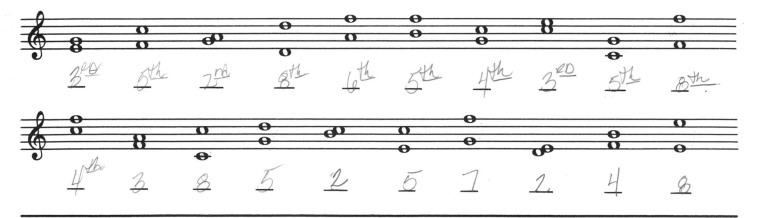

When the notes of the Harmonic Intervals are played separately, they are called MELODIC INTERVALS.

Write NUMBER NAMES for the following MELODIC INTERVALS.

Playing smooth and connected is called ___Legato___.

FDL 737

Lesson No. 15

f is the sign for FORTE which means play loud.

Write *f* below six times.

f f f f f f

---

p is the sign for PIANO which means play soft.

Write *p* below six times.

P P P P P P

Write the number of beats each of the following rests receive in $\frac{4}{4}$ Time or Meter.

4   1   2

A short curved line over or under a group of notes is called a __slur__.

$\frac{2}{4}$ The top number of this Time or Meter Signature indicates there are __2__ beats in each measure.
The bottom number indicates each __quarter__ note receives how many beats? __1__

$\frac{3}{4}$ The top number of this Time or Meter Signature indicates there are __3__ beats in each measure.
The bottom number indicates each __quart__ note receives how many beats? _____

$\frac{4}{4}$ The top number of this Time or Meter Signature indicates there are __4__ beats in each measure.
The bottom number indicates each __quart__ note receives how many beats? _____

An INTERVAL is the distance between __two__ notes.

When the notes of an Interval are played TOGETHER, it is called a __harmonic__ Interval.

When the notes of an Interval are played SEPARATELY, it is called a __melodic__ Interval.

Draw a:

Whole Note.   Half Note.   Quarter Note.   Dotted Half Note.

Another name for Time Signature is __Meter__ Signature.

FDL 737

Lesson No. 16

When notes are on or above the middle line of the staff stems go _down_ on the left.

When notes are below the middle line of the staff stems go _up_ on the right.

Draw stems on the following note heads.

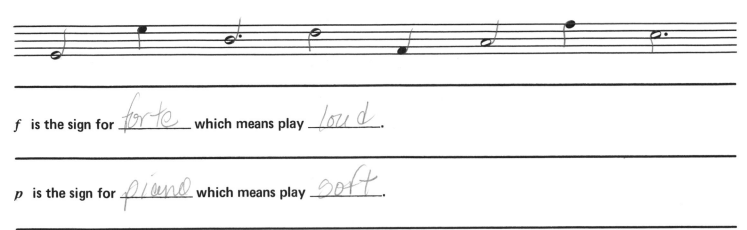

_f_ is the sign for _forte_ which means play _loud_.

_p_ is the sign for _piano_ which means play _soft_.

Draw a:

| Whole Measure Rest. | Half Rest. | Quarter Rest. |

Write the correct letter names for the following notes.

D F G D C C E B A E E A D F

B E C F C F E D A G G E E B

Using Bar Lines divide the following music into measures. Write in the beat counts for each measure.

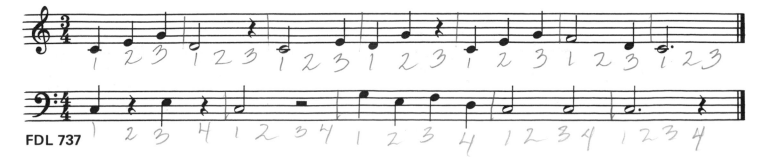

1 2 3 1 2 3 1 2 3 1 2 3 1 2 3 1 2 3 1 2 3

1 2 3 4 1 2 3 4 1 2 3 4 1 2 3 4 1 2 3 4

FDL 737

Lesson No. 17

Add a note to complete each measure of the following music.

Add a rest to complete each measure of the following music.

Write letter names for the following notes of each Harmonic Interval and add its number name. The first one is given.

This is a TIE.

The second note is TIED to the first note. Play the first note only and let it sound for the value of both notes. Only notes on the same degree of the staff can be tied.

Add a TIE line to the following pairs of notes that are on the same degree of the staff.

Under the following pairs of notes write T for Tie and S for Slur.

Lesson No. 18

Draw the notes indicated and add a matching rest on the opposite staff. T.S. means Treble Staff. B.S. means Bass Staff. The first two measures are given.

Use Quarter Notes and Rests.

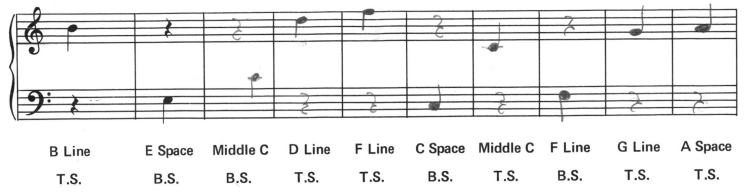

B Line	E Space	Middle C	D Line	F Line	C Space	Middle C	F Line	G Line	A Space
T.S.	B.S.	B.S.	T.S.	T.S.	B.S.	T.S.	B.S.	T.S.	T.S.

Use Half Notes and Rests.

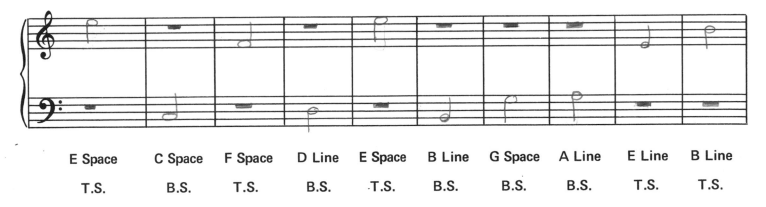

E Space	C Space	F Space	D Line	E Space	B Line	G Space	A Line	E Line	B Line
T.S.	B.S.	T.S.	B.S.	T.S.	B.S.	B.S.	B.S.	T.S.	T.S.

Use Whole Notes and Rests.

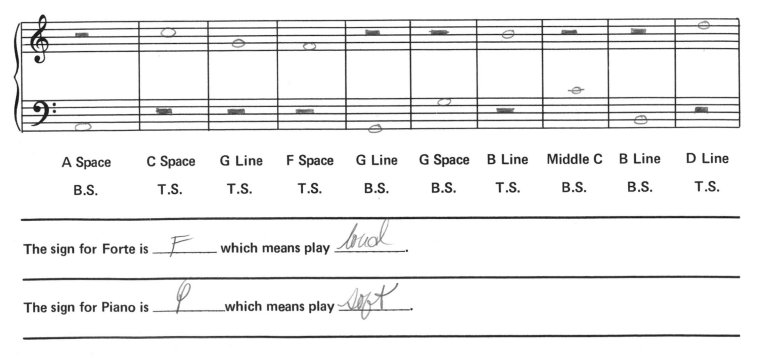

A Space	C Space	G Line	F Space	G Line	G Space	B Line	Middle C	B Line	D Line
B.S.	T.S.	T.S.	T.S.	B.S.	B.S.	T.S.	B.S.	B.S.	T.S.

The sign for Forte is _F_ which means play _loud_.

The sign for Piano is _p_ which means play _soft_.

Playing at a moderate rate of speed is called Moderato. Write the word Moderato below six times.

Moderato, Moderato, Moderato, Moderato, Moderato, Moderato

FDL 737

Lesson No. 19

A long curved line over or under a group of notes that present a complete musical thought is called a PHRASE. A short curved line over or under a group of notes that does not present a complete musical thought is called a SLUR.

Over each curved line in the music below correctly identify them as a PHRASE or SLUR.

When three or more notes are played together, they are called a CHORD.

The first chord below is called the I or Tonic Chord. (C)

The second chord is called the V7 or Dominant Seventh Chord. (G7)

The Roman numerals indicate the degree of the scale upon which the Chord is built. Chord Symbols (letter names) are also given for further clarification. You will learn more about chords and scales in this and other books of this series. The following Chords are in the key of C Major.

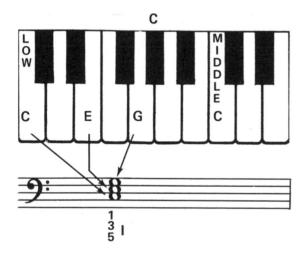

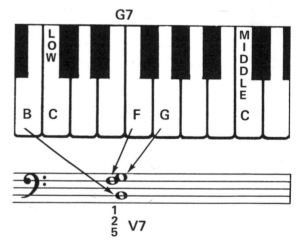

Copy the following I V7 I Chords. They are also known by letter names.

Add TIME SIGNATURES to the music below.

FDL 737

Lesson No. 20

mf is the sign for **MEZZO FORTE** which means play moderately loud. Draw *mf* below six times.

mf mf mf mf mf mf

mp is the sign for **MEZZO PIANO** which means play moderately soft. Draw *mp* below six times.

mp mp mp mp mp mp

Playing at a moderate rate of speed is called _Moderato_.

Add a note to complete each measure of the following music.

Add a rest to complete each measure of the following music.

Write letter names for the following notes of each Melodic Interval and add its number name. The first one is given.

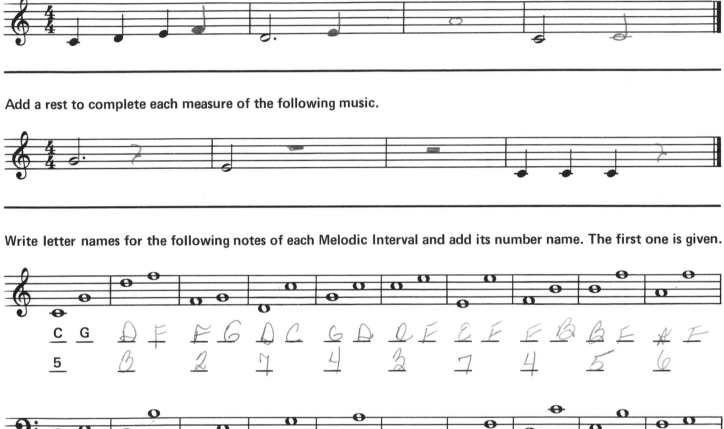

C	G	D	F	E	G	D	C	G	D	D	E	E	F	F	B	B	E	F	E
5		3		2		7		4		3		7		4		5		6	

D	E	C	B	D	E	G	G	A	A	A	C	D	E	D	C	E	B	E	G
2		6		4		8		8		3		5		7		5		2	

Change the following notes as indicated.

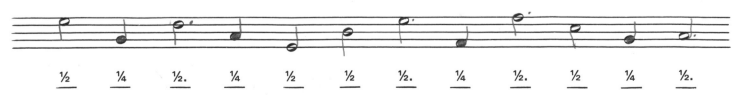

½   ¼   ½.   ¼   ½   ½   ½.   ¼   ½.   ½   ¼   ½.

Lesson No. 21

Draw seven F Clef (Bass Clef) signs.

Draw seven G Clef (Treble Clef) signs.

Write letter names for the following Treble Staff Notes.

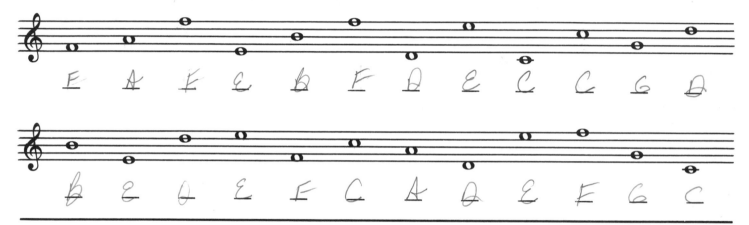

E A E C B F D E C C G A

B E A E F C A A E F G C

Write letter names for the following Bass Staff Notes.

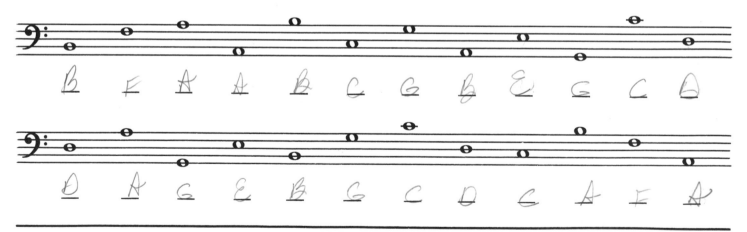

B F A A B C G B E G C A

D A G E B G C D C A E A

Write the I V7 I Chords in the key of C Major.

mf is the sign for _Mezzo forte_ which means play _moderately loudly_ .

mp is the sign for _Mezzo piano_ which means play _moderately softly_ .

Lesson No. 22

This ♭ is a FLAT sign. When it appears before a note, play the very next key <u>down</u> to the left. On a music staff it may appear in a space ‡ or with a line through it ♭ .

Draw Flat signs in the indicated <u>spaces</u>.

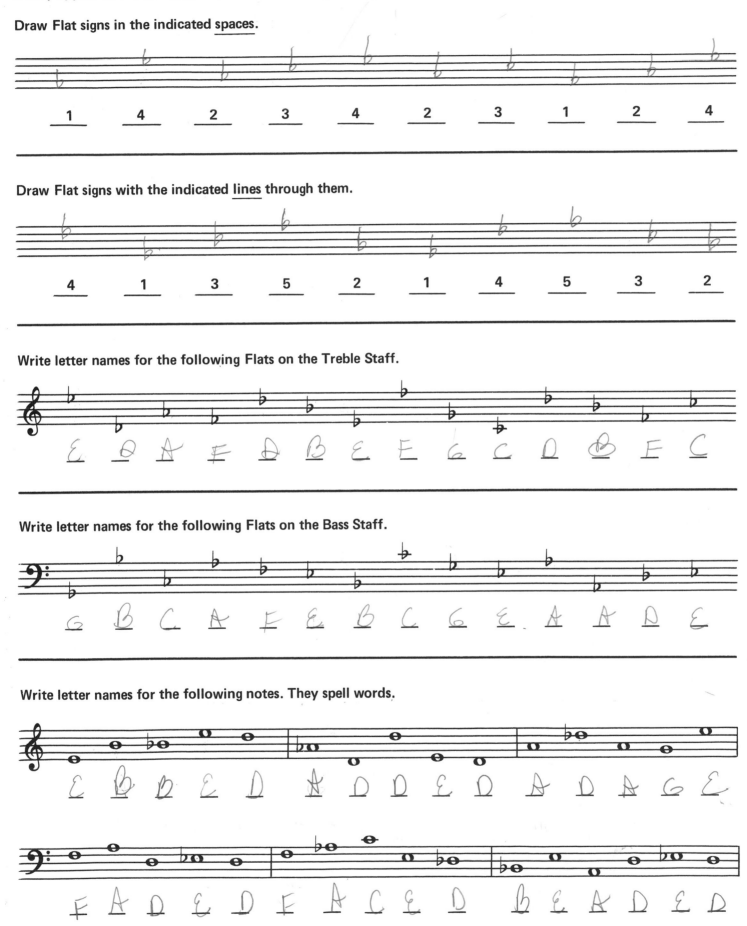

Draw Flat signs with the indicated <u>lines</u> through them.

Write letter names for the following Flats on the Treble Staff.

Write letter names for the following Flats on the Bass Staff.

Write letter names for the following notes. They spell words.

FDL 737

Lesson No. 23

Using Bar Lines divide the following music into measures. Write in the beat counts for each measure.

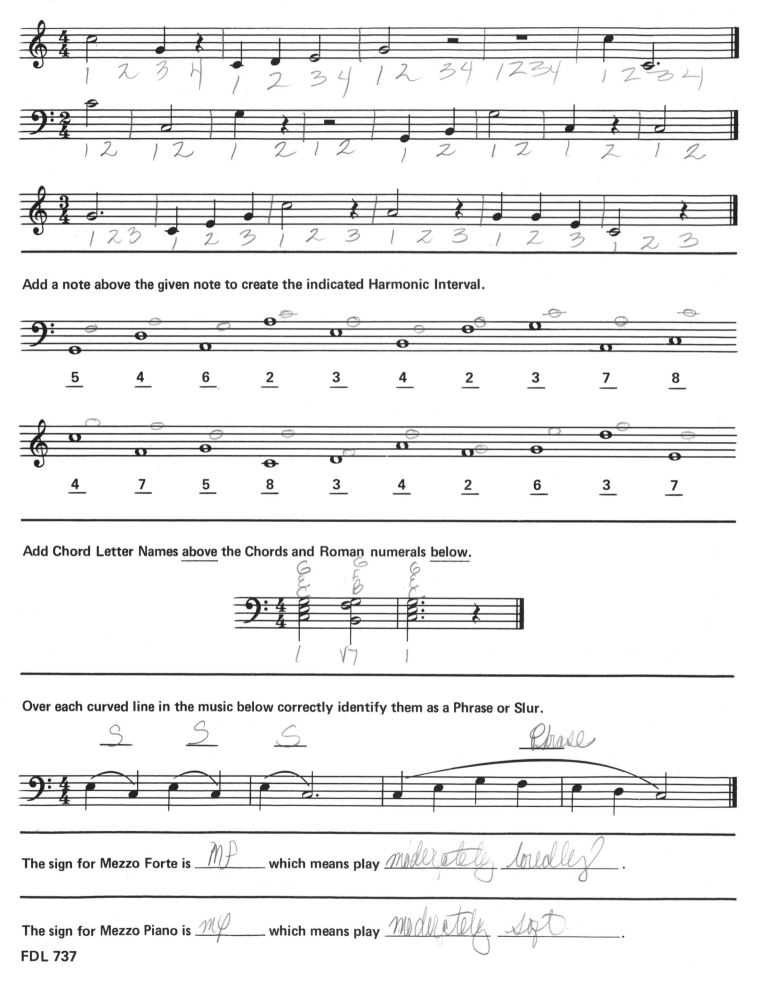

Add a note above the given note to create the indicated Harmonic Interval.

Add Chord Letter Names above the Chords and Roman numerals below.

Over each curved line in the music below correctly identify them as a Phrase or Slur.

The sign for Mezzo Forte is _____ mf _____ which means play _____ moderately loudly _____.

The sign for Mezzo Piano is _____ mp _____ which means play _____ moderately soft _____.

Lesson No. 24

When B♭ is placed at the beginning of a piece it means all Bs are to be played flat. B♭ is the KEY SIGNATURE for the key of F MAJOR.

Copy the above F MAJOR KEY SIGNATURE.

Write letter names for the following notes in the key of F Major.

C B♭ D B♭ C E G B D E F B♭ A C

D E B♭ C G B B♭ B A E C B G A

The Chords you have learned so far have been in the key of C Major. The following Chords are in the key of F Major.

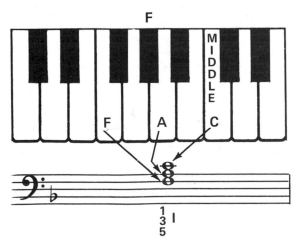

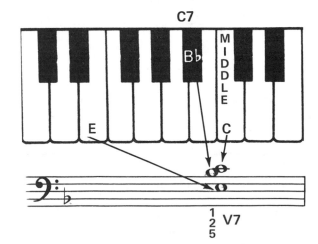

Copy the following I V7 I Chords. They are also known by letter names.

FDL 737

26

Lesson No. 25

Rit. is the abbreviation for RITARDANDO which means gradually slower. Write rit. below six times.

Rit Rit Rit Rit Rit Rit

Playing at a walking speed is called ANDANTE. Write the word Andante below six times.

Andante Andante Andante Andante Andante Andante

Add Chord Letter Names above the chords and Roman numerals below.

I   V7   V7.

Under the following pairs of notes write T for Tie and S for Slur.

S   T   T   S   S

Legato means to play *smooth* and *connected*.

Draw stems on the following note heads.

Playing at a lively speed is called ANIMATO. Write the word Animato six times.

Animato, Animato, Animato, Animato, Animato, Animato

Draw Whole Notes as indicated.

G Line	C Space	F Line	A Space	B Line	E Space	B Space	D Line	G Space	A Line

This 𝄻 is a *whole* Measure Rest. In 4/4 Time or Meter it receives *4* beats. In 3/4 Time or Meter it receives *3* beats.

FDL 737

Lesson No. 26

Complete the Grand Staff and add the F Major Key Signature.

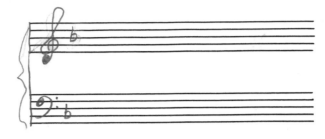

Write the I V7 I Chords in the key of F Major.

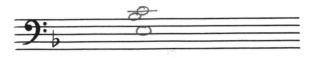

Draw two _line_ notes for each given letter name. Place one on Bass Staff and one on Treble Staff. Use Half Notes. The first two are given.

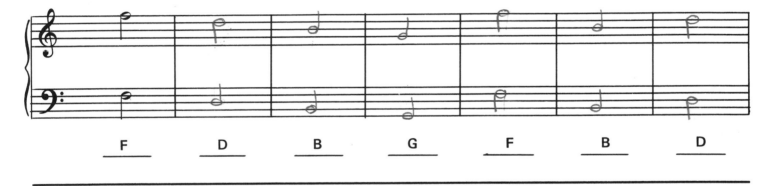

F   D   B   G   F   B   D

Draw two _space_ notes for each given letter name. Place one on Bass Staff and one on Treble Staff. Use Quarter Notes.

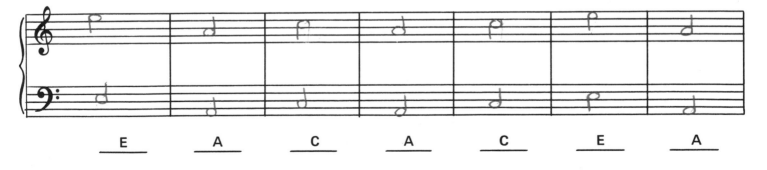

E   A   C   A   C   E   A

Write letter names for the following notes in the key of F Major.

C B E B C B D B G G B E A A

FDL 737

Lesson No. 27

This ♯ is a SHARP sign. When it appears before a note, play the very next key up to the right. On a music staff it may appear in a space ♯ or with a line through it ♯ . Draw Sharp signs in the indicated spaces.

4   1   3   4   2   1   2   3   2   1

Draw Sharp signs with the indicated lines through them.

1   4   2   3   1   5   2   3   5   4

Write letter names for the following Sharps on the Treble Staff.

D D A F B E C F E G C A G E

Write letter names for the following Sharps on the Bass Staff.

B C E E E C E A D F A C B C

Write letter names for the following notes. They spell words.

E D G E   B E G   F E E D   F E D

D E E D   B E F   E G G   F A C E

Lesson No. 28

When F♯ is placed at the beginning of a piece it means all Fs are to be played sharp. F♯ is the KEY SIGNATURE for the key of G MAJOR.

Copy the above G MAJOR KEY SIGNATURE.

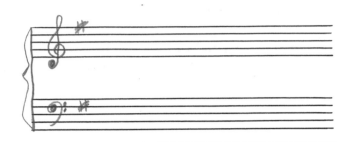

Write letter names for the following notes in the key of G Major.

C   G   C   E   D   A   D   E   B   E   F   D   E   E

C   E   B   C   E   A   F   D   G   G   D   E   A   B

The Chords you have learned so far have been in the key of C Major and F Major. The following Chords are in the key of G Major.

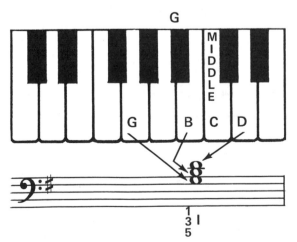

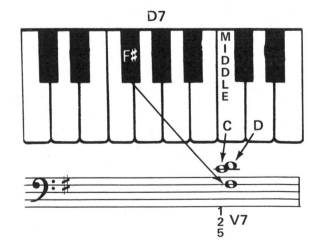

Copy the following I V7 I Chords. They are also known by letter names.

Lesson No. 29

A dot above  or below a note means to play detached not connected. This is called STACCATO. Add Staccato dots to the following notes.

Playing not too fast but moving along is called ALLEGRETTO. Write the word Allegretto below six times.

allegretto, allegretto, allegretto, allegretto, allegretto, allegretto

Add Chord Letter Names above the Chords and Roman numerals below.

Key of C Major	Key of F Major	Key of G Major
Key Signature - No Sharps or Flats	Key Signature - B Flat	Key Signature - F Sharp

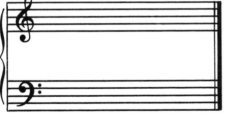

Copy the above below.

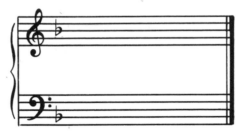

Write letter names for the following notes in the key of G Major.

Lesson No. 30

The abbreviation for Ritardando is _Rit_ which means _gradually slower_.

Andante means to play at a _walking_ speed.

Write the I V7 I Chords in the key of G Major.

Animato means to play at a _lively_ speed.

Playing smooth and connected is called _legato_.

Moderato means to play at a _moderate_ speed.

Playing not too fast but moving along is called _allegretto_.

Write letter names for the following LINE notes.

G B D F A C C E G B D F

Write letter names for the following SPACE notes.

A C E G B D E A G C

Allegretto means to play not too _fast_ but _moving along_.

FDL 737

Lesson No. 31

When a flag is added to a Quarter Note it becomes an EIGHTH NOTE.

When the stem is <u>up</u> the flag appears this way ♪ .

When the stem is <u>down</u> the flag appears this way ♭ .

Change the following Quarter Notes to Eighth Notes.

When the ²⁄₄ , ³⁄₄ , or ⁴⁄₄ Time Signature is used the Eighth Note receives ½ of a beat. This ⅞ is an EIGHTH REST. It has the same beat value as one Eighth Note. Draw six Eighth Rests below.

Eighth Notes may appear in pairs ♫ or in groups ♬ . When this occurs they are joined together by a BEAM.

Change the following pairs of Quarter Notes to Eighth Notes.

Change the following groups of Quarter Notes to Eighth Notes.

Two Eighth Notes have the same beat value as one Quarter Note.

Using Bar Lines divide the following music into measures. Write in the beat counts for each measure. The first two measures are given.

FDL 737

Lesson No. 32

Added lines and spaces for notes above and below the music staff are called LEGER LINES and SPACES.

B C D E notes <u>above</u> Bass Staff.

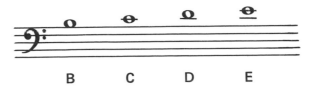

B   C   D   E

Write letter names for the following notes.

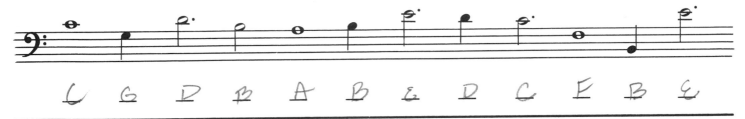

C   G   D   B   A   B   E   D   C   E   B   E

D C B A notes <u>below</u> Treble Staff.

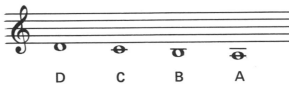

D   C   B   A

Write letter names for the following notes.

D   E   B   A   C   D   E   C   A   G   C   B

Write letter names for the following notes.

D   D   B   C   E   E   A   B   E   A   D   G   C   B   E   A

A   D   B   D   B   C   A   D   D   E   A   E   D   C   E   G

FDL 737

34

Lesson No. 33

G A B C notes **above** Treble Staff.

G   A   B   C

Write letter names for the following notes.

C A G B C A E C B G E C

F E D C notes **below** Bass Staff.

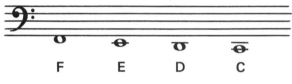

F   E   D   C

Write letter names for the following notes.

F D C C E A D E G C B E

Write letter names for the following notes.

G C B C A D G E C B D C A B E B

C F D C E E C D F B D B A E D A

FDL 737

Lesson No. 34

Playing music in a different key from that in which it is written is called TRANSPOSING.

The following melody is shown two ways. It is first presented in the key of C Major then TRANSPOSED when presented in the key of F Major.

C Major

F Major

Notice the first note. It is C, the same as its key signature. Also notice how it steps up then skips down ending on the note of C.

When Transposed notice the first note. It is F, the same as its key signature. Also notice how it steps up then skips down ending on the note of F.

IMPORTANT: In both keys the pattern of steps and skips is the same; however, the notes are different.

Transpose the following melody from C Major to F Major.

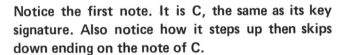

Transpose the following melody from F Major to C Major.

Transpose the following melody from C Major to G Major.

Playing at a fast speed is called ALLEGRO. Write the word Allegro below six times.

Allegro   Allegro   Allegro   Allegro   Allegro   Allegro

This > is an ACCENT MARK. When it appears above or below a note it means to play that note <u>loud</u>. Draw Accent Marks for the following notes.

This ⁷ is an Eighth Rest. It has the same beat value as one *eighth* note.

Eighth Notes in pairs are joined together by a *bar*.

FDL 737

Lesson No. 35

The DAMPER PEDAL sustains tones:

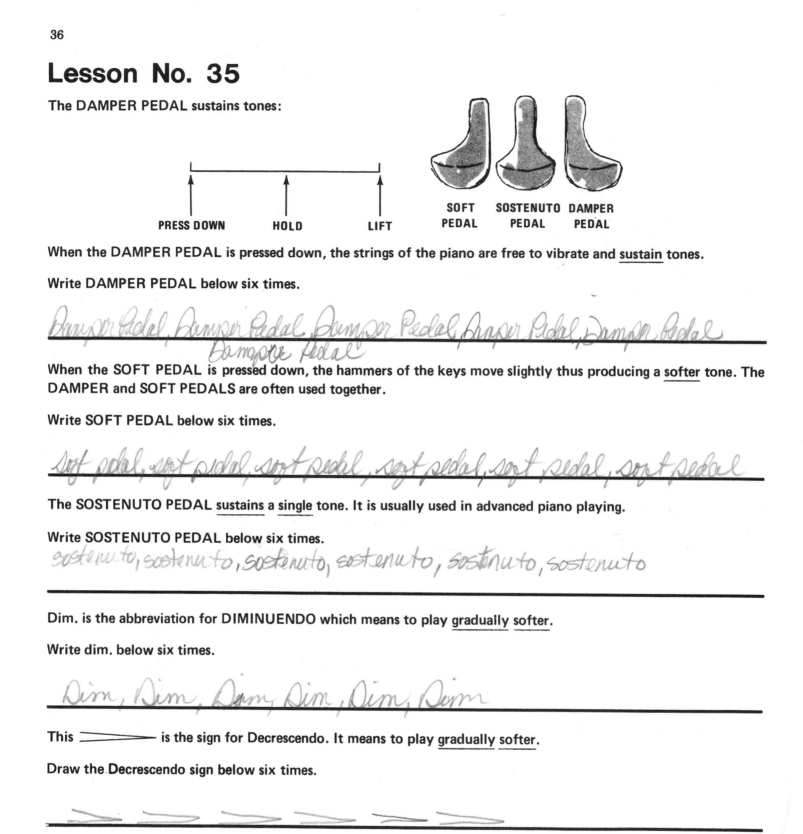

PRESS DOWN   HOLD   LIFT

SOFT PEDAL   SOSTENUTO PEDAL   DAMPER PEDAL

When the DAMPER PEDAL is pressed down, the strings of the piano are free to vibrate and <u>sustain</u> tones.

Write DAMPER PEDAL below six times.

Damper Pedal, Damper Pedal, Damper Pedal, Damper Pedal, Damper Pedal, Damper Pedal

When the SOFT PEDAL is pressed down, the hammers of the keys move slightly thus producing a <u>softer</u> tone. The DAMPER and SOFT PEDALS are often used together.

Write SOFT PEDAL below six times.

soft pedal, soft pedal, soft pedal, soft pedal, soft pedal, soft pedal

The SOSTENUTO PEDAL <u>sustains</u> a <u>single</u> tone. It is usually used in advanced piano playing.

Write SOSTENUTO PEDAL below six times.

sostenuto, sostenuto, sostenuto, sostenuto, sostenuto, sostenuto

Dim. is the abbreviation for DIMINUENDO which means to play <u>gradually</u> softer.

Write dim. below six times.

Dim, Dim, Dim, Dim, Dim, Dim

This ▭ is the sign for Decrescendo. It means to play <u>gradually</u> softer.

Draw the Decrescendo sign below six times.

Cresc. is the abbreviation for CRESCENDO which means to play <u>gradually</u> louder.

Write cresc. below six times.

Cresc, Cresc, Cresc, Cresc, Cresc, Cresc

This ◁ is the sign for Crescendo. It means to play <u>gradually</u> louder.

Draw the Crescendo sign below six times.

FDL 737

Lesson No. 36

When notes of a chord are played one after the other instead of together, they are called an ARPEGGIO. The word Arpeggio comes from the Italian word <u>arpeggiare</u>, meaning to play upon a harp.

Write the word Arpeggio below six times.

Arpeggio, Arpeggio, Arpeggio, Arpeggio, Arpeggio, Arpeggio

Copy the following C Major Arpeggio. It is built on the I Chord.

Write the G Major Arpeggio built on the I Chord below. Use the above C Major Arpeggio as an example. The first note is given.

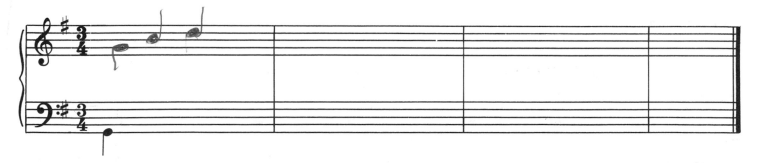

Write the F Major Arpeggio built on the I Chord below. The first note is given.

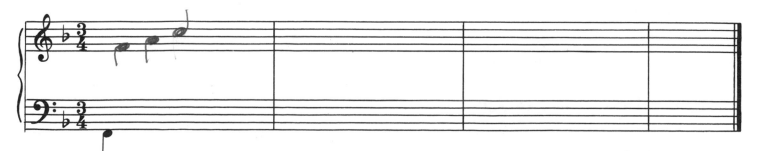

FDL 737

Lesson No. 37

The following music is in the key of _____C_____ Major. Transpose it to the key of F Major.

This > is an *decrescendo* mark. When it appears above or below a note it means to play that note *softer*.

Allegro means to play at a *fast* speed.

When the $\frac{2}{4}$, $\frac{3}{4}$, or $\frac{4}{4}$ Time Signature is used the Eighth Note receives how many beats. *2* Two Eighth Notes have the same beat value as one *quarter* note.

When notes of a chord are played one after the other instead of together, they are called an *arpeggio*

When the *damper* pedal is pressed down, the strings of the piano are free to vibrate and sustain tones.

When the *soft* pedal is pressed down, the hammers of the keys move slightly thus producing a *softer* tone.

The *sostenuto* pedal sustains a single tone. It is usually used in advanced piano playing.

What is the Key Signature for the key of G Major? *b flat*

What is the Key Signature for the key of C Major? _____

What is the Key Signature for the key of F Major? *f sharp*

The abbreviation for Diminuendo is *Dim* which means *gradually softer*.

Lesson No. 38

This ♮ is a NATURAL sign. It cancels a sharp or flat when it appears before a note. On a music staff it may appear in a space ♮ or with a line through it ♮ .

Draw Natural signs in the indicated spaces.

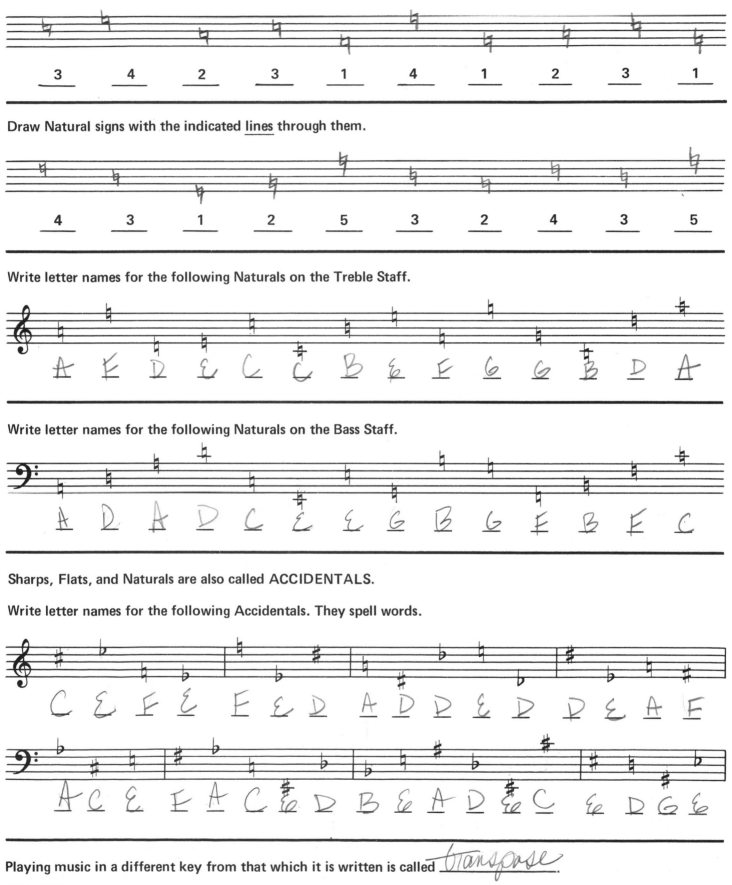

| 3 | 4 | 2 | 3 | 1 | 4 | 1 | 2 | 3 | 1 |

Draw Natural signs with the indicated lines through them.

| 4 | 3 | 1 | 2 | 5 | 3 | 2 | 4 | 3 | 5 |

Write letter names for the following Naturals on the Treble Staff.

A E D E C C B E E G G B D A

Write letter names for the following Naturals on the Bass Staff.

A D A D C E E G B G E B E C

Sharks, Flats, and Naturals are also called ACCIDENTALS.

Write letter names for the following Accidentals. They spell words.

C E F E   E E D   A D D E D   D E A F

A C E   F A C E D   B E A D   C   E D G E

Playing music in a different key from that which it is written is called _transpose_

Lesson No. 39

Playing detached and not connected is called _staccato_.

This ───── is the sign for _decrescendo_. It means to play _grad. softer_.

This ───── is the sign for _Crescendo_. It means to play _grad. louder_.

The following music is in the key of ___F___ Major. Transpose it to the key of G Major.

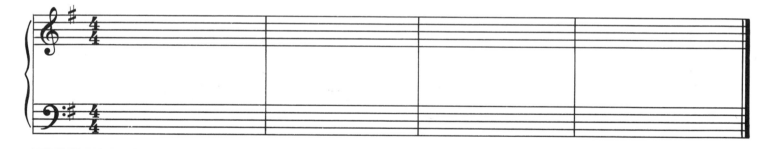

A dot placed <u>after</u> a note adds <u>half</u> the value of the note it follows.

$\frac{2}{4}$ — $\frac{3}{4}$ — $\frac{4}{4}$ Time Signature

DOTTED HALF NOTE ♩. receives 3 Beats.

DOTTED QUARTER NOTE ♩. receives 1½ Beats.

Using Bar Lines divide the following music into measures. Write in the beat counts for each measure using this mark + for the half beat. The first two measures are given.

Lesson No. 40

Da Capo al Fine means return to the beginning and play to the word Fine. The abbreviation for Da Capo al Fine is D. C. al Fine. Write this abbreviation below six times.

D.C. al Fine, D.C. al Fine, D.C. al Fine, D.C. al Fine, D.C. al Fine,
D.C. al Fine

The keyboard has Half Steps and Whole Steps. From one key to the very next key is a Half Step. From one to another with one key in between is a Whole Step.

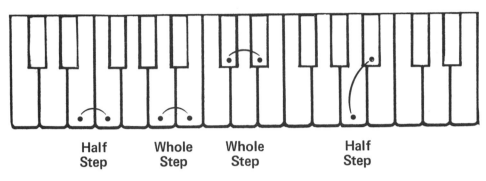

Half Step   Whole Step   Whole Step   Half Step

Under the marked keys write H for Half and W for Whole.

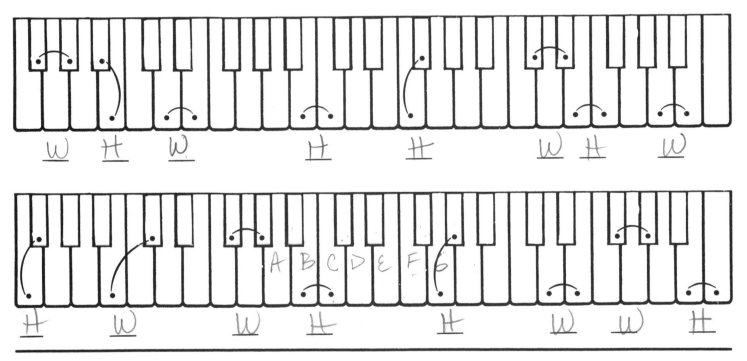

W   H   W   H   H   W   H   W

H   W   W   H   H   W   W   H

Under the following pairs of notes write W for those that form Whole Steps and H for those that form Half Steps.

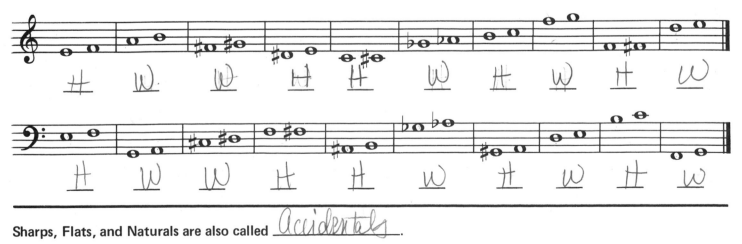

H   W   W   H   H   W   H   W   H   W

H   W   W   H   H   W   H   W   H   W

Sharps, Flats, and Naturals are also called <u>Accidentals</u>.

FDL 737

Lesson No. 41

A TETRACHORD is two Whole Steps and a Half Step arranged as follows.

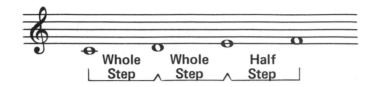

Write the word Tetrachord below six times.

Tetrachord, Tetrachord, Tetracherd, Tetrachord, Tetrachord, Tetracherd

By adding sharps or flats when necessary change the following groups of notes to Tetrachords. In the brackets below the notes write W for Whole Step and H for Half Step. Remember they must be arranged in this pattern: Whole Step — Whole Step — Half Step. The first Tetrachord is given.

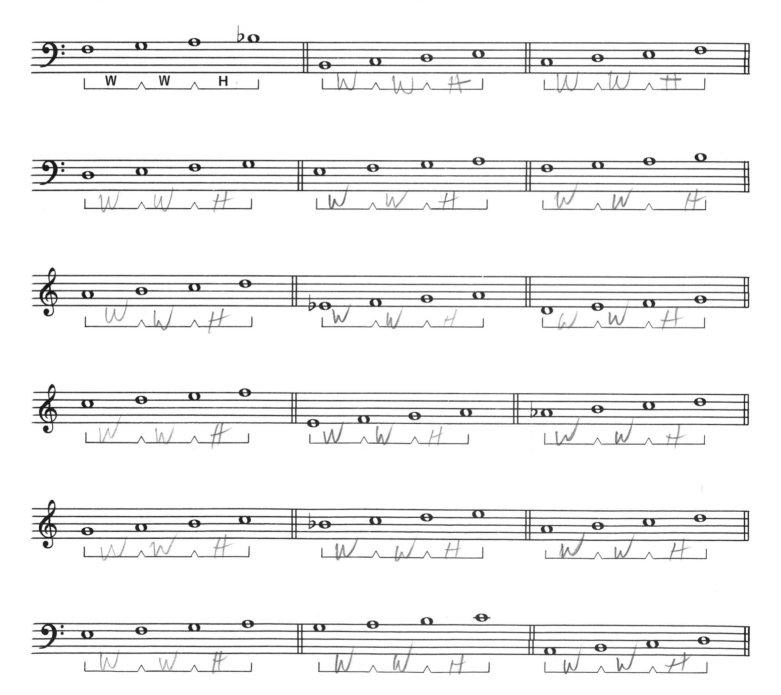

Lesson No. 42

Two Tetrachords divided by a Whole Step form a Major Scale.

C MAJOR SCALE

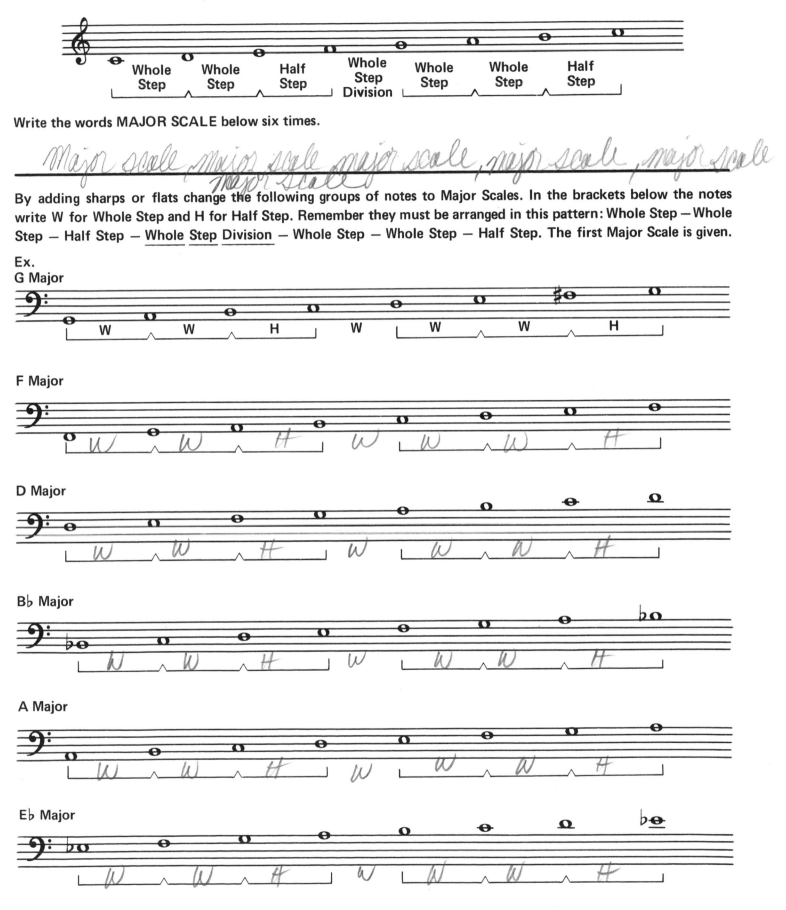

Write the words MAJOR SCALE below six times.

Major scale, major scale, major scale, major scale, major scale
Major Scale

By adding sharps or flats change the following groups of notes to Major Scales. In the brackets below the notes write W for Whole Step and H for Half Step. Remember they must be arranged in this pattern: Whole Step — Whole Step — Half Step — Whole Step Division — Whole Step — Whole Step — Half Step. The first Major Scale is given.

Ex.
G Major

W   W   H   W   W   W   H

F Major

W   W   H   W   W   W   H

D Major

W   W   H   W   W   W   H

B♭ Major

W   W   H   W   W   W   H

A Major

W   W   H   W   W   W   H

E♭ Major

W   W   H   W   W   W   H

FDL 737

Lesson No. 43

C is another way to indicate the **4/4** Time Signature. It is called COMMON TIME. Draw three more Common Time Signatures like the one given below.

When moving from the I Chord to the V7 Chord, the bottom note moves <u>down</u> one-half step, the middle note moves <u>up</u> one-half step, and the top note <u>remains</u> the same. Add the following V7 Chords below.

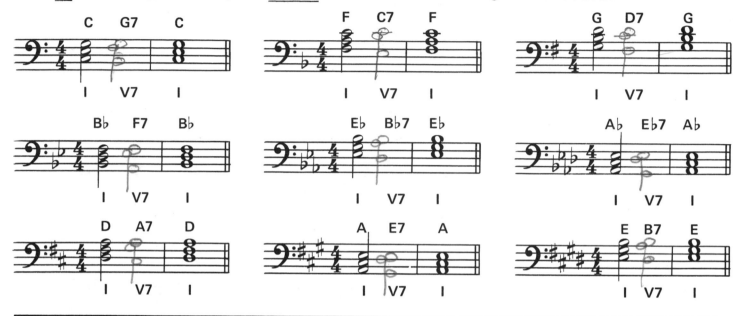

 This is a REPEAT SIGN. It indicates a certain part or the entire piece is to be played again.

Draw four Repeat Signs below.

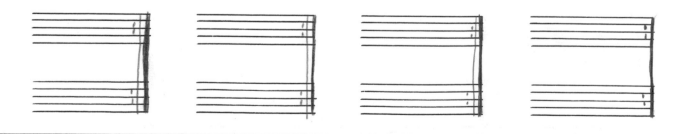

The sign *a tempo* means to return to the original speed. Write *a tempo* below six times.

a tempo, a tempo, a tempo, a tempo, a tempo, a tempo

A dot placed after a note adds ___1/2___ the value of the note it follows.

Playing music in a different key from that which it is written is called ___transpose___.

FDL 737

Lesson No. 44

Adding another major chord to the two chords you know, I and V7, will enable you to play many more nes.
This chord is called the IV or SUBDOMINANT CHORD. Copy the following I, IV, I, V7, I Chords.

When moving from the I Chord to the IV Chord, the bottom note <u>remains</u> the same, the middle note moves <u>up</u>
one-half step, and the top note moves <u>up</u> one whole step.

Add the following IV Chords below.

Dal Segno al Fine means return to the sign (𝄋) and play to the word Fine. The abbreviation for Dal Segno al
Fine is D. S. al Fine. Write the abbreviation below six times.

D.S. al Fine, D.S. al Fine, D.S. al Fine, D.S. al Fine, D.S. al Fine, D.S. al Fine.

When you return to the original speed it is called *a tempo*.

FDL 737

Lesson No. 45

A Tetrachord is 2 whole steps and a half step.

A Major Scale has 2 Tetrachords divided by a whole step.

Write Key Signatures for the given keys below.

G Major

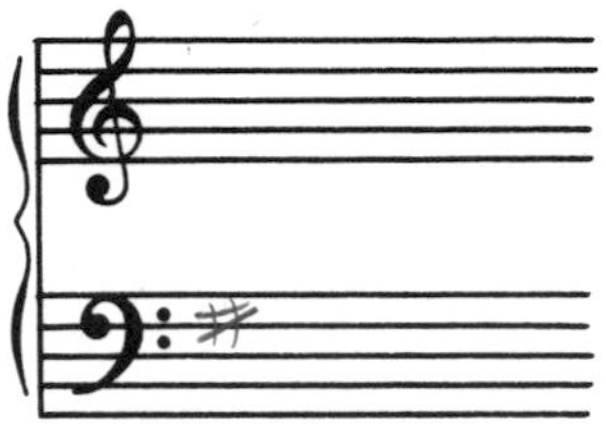

F Major

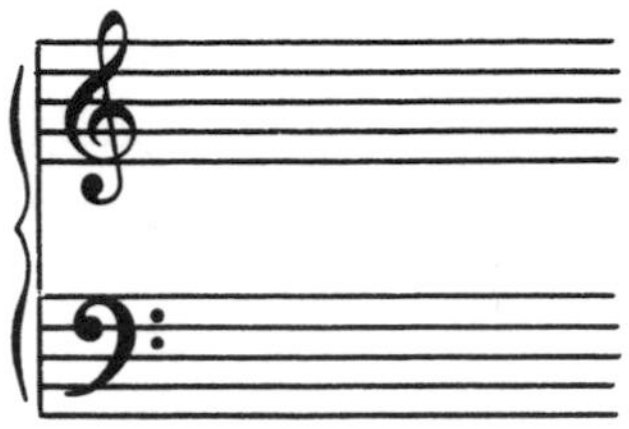

D Major

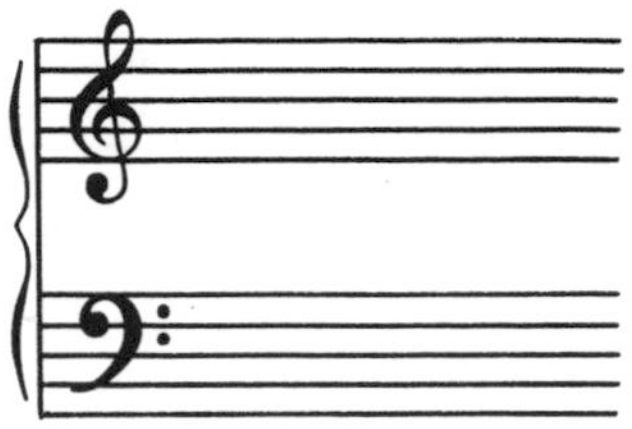

B♭ Major

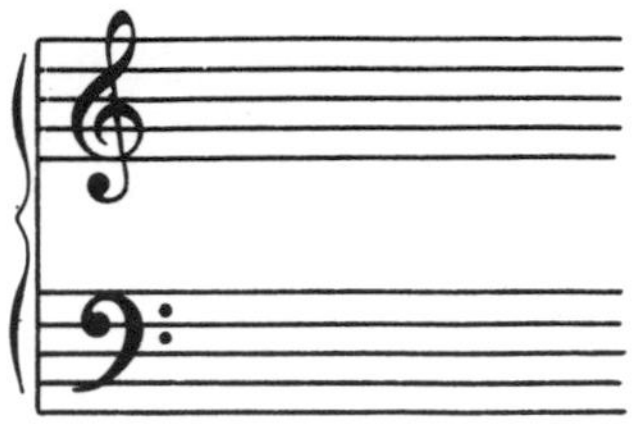

A Major

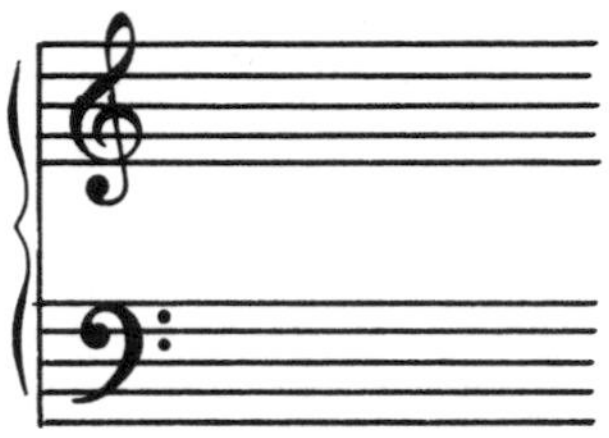

E♭ Major

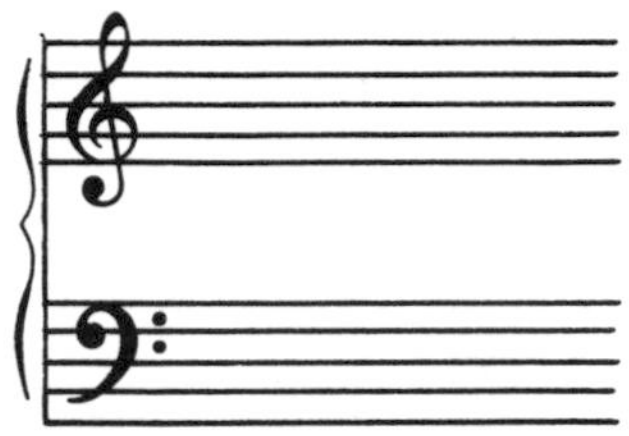

E Major

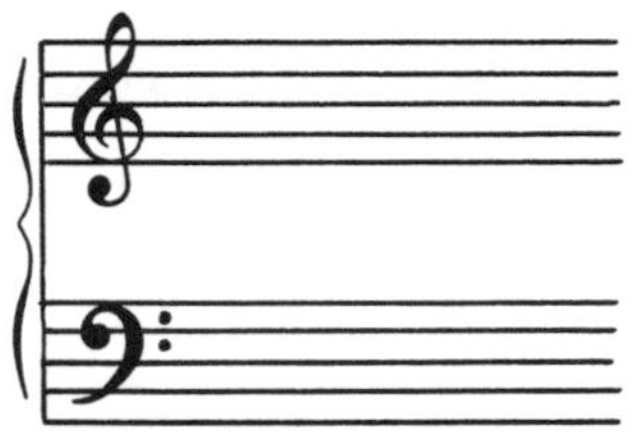

A♭ Major

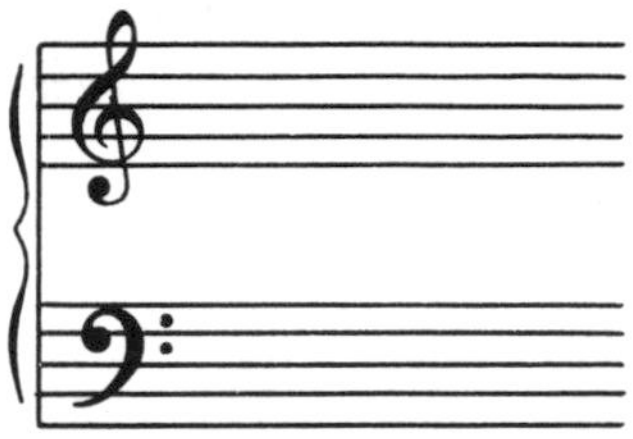

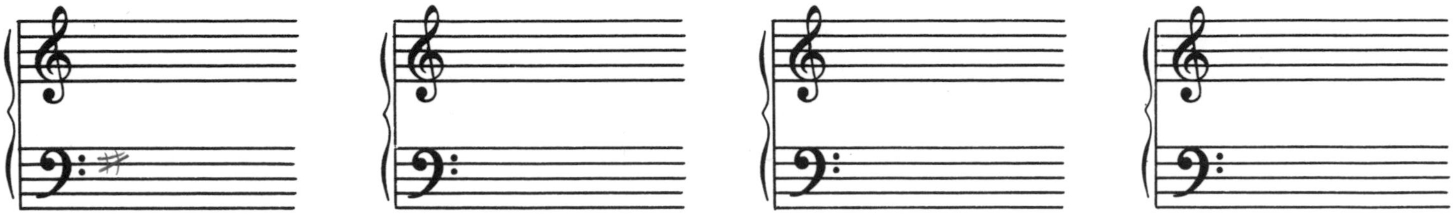

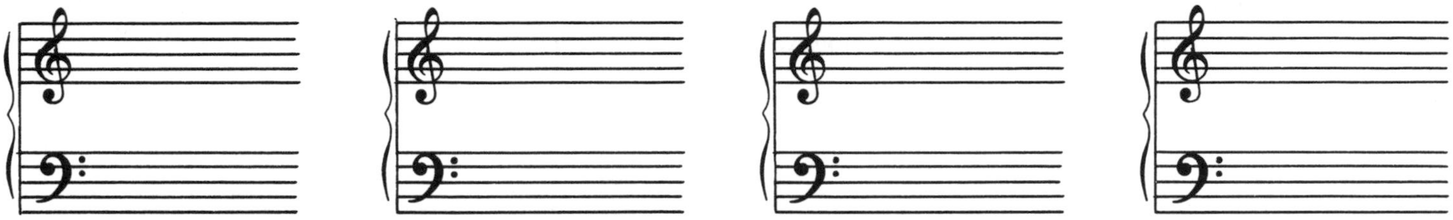

6/8 The top number of this TIME or METER SIGNATURE indicates SIX beats in each measure. The bottom number indicates each EIGHTH NOTE receives ONE beat.

Draw four 6/8 Time or Meter Signatures on the staff below.

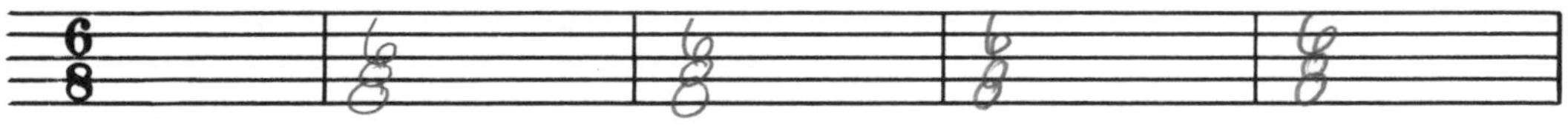

When the 6/8 Time Signature is used the notes and rests below receive the following beat value.

NOTES	BEATS	RESTS
♪	1	𝄾
♩	2	𝄽
♩.	3	𝄽.
𝅗𝅥.	6	𝄽. 𝄽. (𝄼)

Write the beat counts for the following music. The first measure is given.

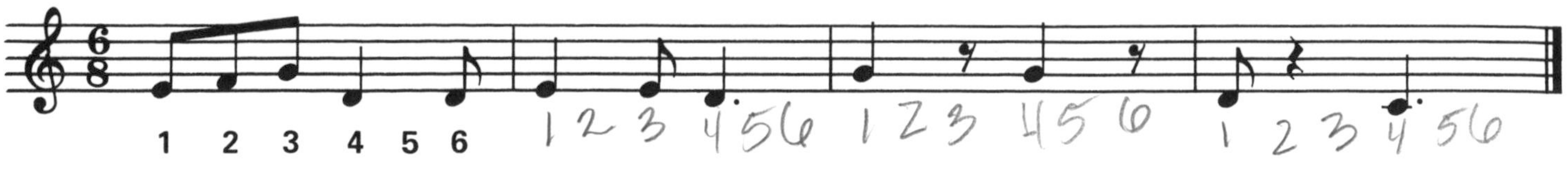

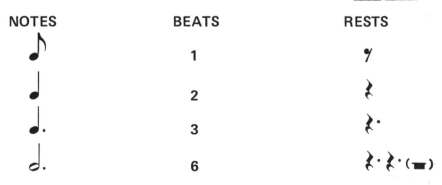

Lesson No. 46

The abbreviation for Dal Segno al Fine is *D.S. al Fine*. It means return to the *S.* and play to the word *Fine* .

$\frac{6}{8}$ The top number of this Time or Meter Signature indicates there are _____ beats in each measure.
The bottom number indicates each _____ note receives how many beats? _____

This ⌢ is a FERMATA sign. When it appears above ⌢ or below ⌣ a note, hold the note slightly longer than its given beat value.

Write the word FERMATA below six times.

Fermata, Fermata, Fermata, Fermata, Fermata, Fermata

Draw a Fermata sign <u>above</u> each of the following notes.

Draw a Fermata sign <u>below</u> each of the following notes.

The following music is in the key of *C* Major. Transpose it to the key of D Major.

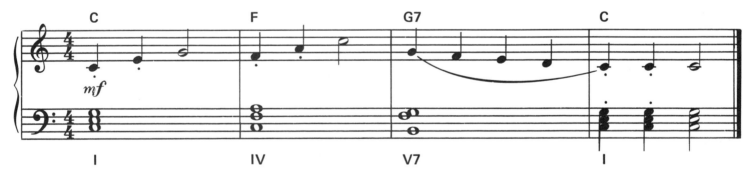

The beat value of this note ♪ in $\frac{6}{8}$ Time or Meter is *1* .

The beat value of this note ♪ in $\frac{4}{4}$ Time or Meter is *2* .

FDL 737

Lesson No. 47

Write the number of beats each of the following notes receive in **6/8** Time or Meter.

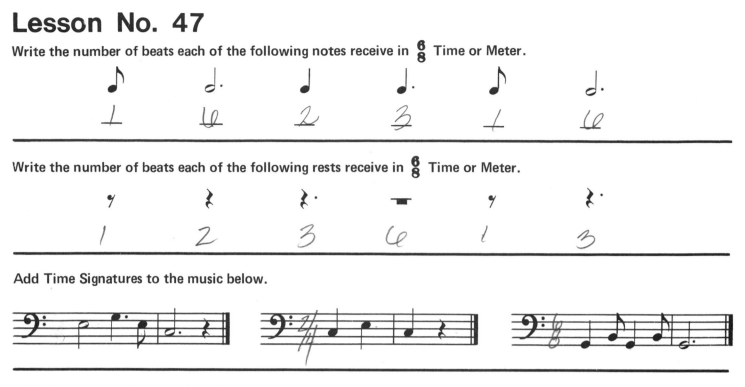

Write the number of beats each of the following rests receive in **6/8** Time or Meter.

Add Time Signatures to the music below.

Add Chord Letter Names <u>above</u> the Chords and Roman numerals <u>below</u>.

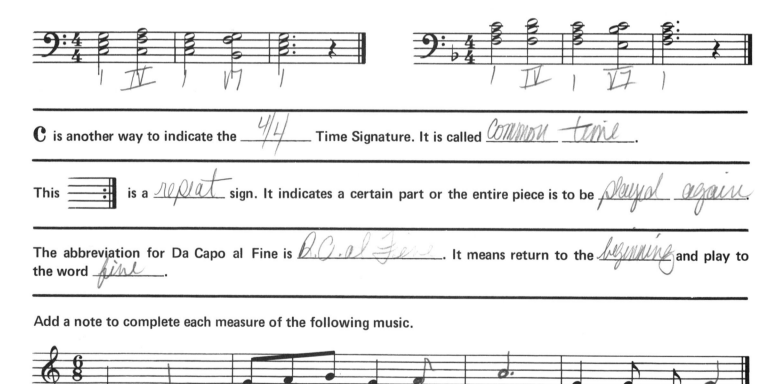

C is another way to indicate the ___4/4___ Time Signature. It is called _Common time_.

This 𝄇 is a _repeat_ sign. It indicates a certain part or the entire piece is to be _played again_.

The abbreviation for Da Capo al Fine is _D.C. al Fine_. It means return to the _beginning_ and play to the word _fine_.

Add a note to complete each measure of the following music.

Add a rest to complete each measure of the following music.

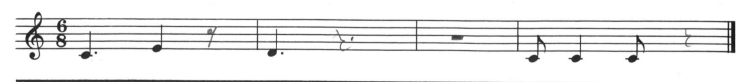

This 𝄐 is a _Fermatta_ sign. When it appears above or below a note, hold the note slightly _longer_ than its given beat value.

FDL 737